Life & Times of a Honky Tonk Drummer

By

Troy Benton (Skeet) Seaton

Copyright © 2012

By Troy B. Skeet Seaton

All Rights Reserved.

Dedication

I would like to dedicate this book to my parents, A.G. and Eunice Seaton, whose love and support, as well as encouragement allowed me to become involved, at a very early age, at what has become my passion.

This book is also dedicated to my lovely wife, Rose Seaton, who has been by my side for the last ten years, seeing me through all things good and bad, not just my music, but my life in general. She is also responsible for encouraging me to write this book.

Acknowledgements

Morse Gist

Stan Balch

Sonny Payne

Jim Howe

Lil Henry Edgin

John Pope

Jimmy Rogers

C.W. Gatlin

Butch Carter

Tom Mathis

Allen Snider

Larry Shirley (gone but not forgotten)

Jimmy Allen AKA Tonto

Memorial Page

This page is dedicated to all the musicians I have known or played with who have gone on to the big band stand in the sky. They are gone but not forgotten, for their music will live on in our hearts and minds forever.

Mack Self   RHOF

Jimmy Evans   RHOF

Levon Helm   RRHOF

Sonny "Red" Baker

Don Nicholas

Bobby Ervin

Jimmy Snyder

Roger Hawkins

Otis Wake

John "Buttermilk" Huey

David Bryant

Larry Shirley

Gary Summerhill

Glen Brown

About the Author

My name is Skeet Seaton (Troy Benton Seaton), and I was born into a musical family on October 8th 1952, in Wynne, Arkansas. My grandfather played trumpet, my father played six different instruments, and my uncle played upright bass, sang and did what at the time was called black face comedy. At the age of eight my Dad and his brother had their own radio show and were working musicians (Seaton Hot Shots).

When I was 2 years old, my family moved to Lexa, Arkansas, which had a direct bearing on my musical interest and afforded me the good fortune to play with some of the best musicians in the Delta. We moved to West Helena when I was five years old, and at age eight I began to have an interest in playing drums. My Dad and other local musicians would play at house parties. It was a big deal in the fifties. I would go along and thus began my exciting and fun filled journey along music's highway.
My first drum was a Slingerland snare drum in Tobacco Sunburst. Man, I wish I still had that! I took lessons for a brief time at Gist Music Company. It didn't take long for my Dad to realize that my instructor might be ok on some things, but drums were not one of them. I had a brief period of time from age 9 to 11 that I lost interest. Then Rock and Roll (The Beatles, Stones, the Band) hit the airwaves and I knew music was calling me back. My first drums were a set of E.W. Kent's. They were gold sparkle and I was as proud of them as if they were Ludwigs.

We formed a Rock & Roll band (Allen Snider, Jimmy Allen, Larry Shirley and myself.) Wild names were in so we became (are you ready for this?) "The Mellow Street Syndicate." It sounded really cool then, but looking back, I just don't know. We played some teen parties and a few gigs along the way like most budding musicians, and it was a lot of fun. I took band in school and had a band director (Stan Balch) who not only was a knock-your-socks-off director but a great musician in his own right. I later had the pleasure of playing in a combo with him as well as Sonny Payne (the legendary host of King Biscuit Time radio show on KFFA radio station) on the upright bass, and Steve Alsup (band director) on piano. We played nothing newer than 1945, all acoustic, no vocals. It was a great learning experience, not to mention the fact that we had a blast.

At the age of 16, I got hooked in with some really seasoned club musicians from this area. They ranged in age from 27 to 42. At first I thought it might not work with the club owner, but we got past that. Now came the real hurdle (my Mom.) We were booked in a club called the Delta Supper Club. This club is where many greats honed their skills and went on to become major entertainers. Conway Twitty, Levon Helm, Ace Cannon, Ronnie Hawkins, just to name a few. Well, when I got home I didn't know how to approach this situation, but I sure was glad to see my Dad home from work. It seemed to tilt things a little more my way. You have to take into account I was a kid in high school asking to go into a den of sin three nights a week.

Well, as I figured, my Mom was not nearly as excited about this wonderful opportunity as I was. This is where my trump card paid off. My Dad said we should sit down and talk about it before we made a decision. (He had been playing in clubs at the age of ten.) Of course, it was a lot different in 1935. My Mom finally gave in, but it came with a long list of conditions. First, I couldn't let my grades fall (there wasn't much room for that anyway.) We finished at 1 A.M. and I had to be home by 1:30 A.M. and positively no booze. I was making double the amount in one night that my friends made bagging groceries at the local grocery store in a week.

The Supper Club was built in the 40's and over the years they put a salvage yard around it. It was a very fun place that drew people from all around. A lot of people referred to it in later years as the "Junk Yard."

Growing up in Phillips County exposed me to a wide variety of musical styles that you just didn't hear in some areas. You had live blues greats Sonny Boy Williamson, Frank Frost, Sam Carr and many more. Also there were country, rockabilly, and rock and roll greats from Phillips County like Conway Twitty (Harold Jenkins), Levon Helm, Mack Self, C.W. Gatlin, Jimmy Evans, just to name a few. They all made their mark, both here and abroad. It was a young musician's dream to grow up surrounded by all that talent. I have been very blessed to have played with most of the people mentioned, as well a long list of those not mentioned.

Skeet Seaton, The Early Years

Live Wire Band 2012
Little Henry Edgin, Jimmy Rogers,
Skeet Seaton, John Pope

I got my first paying gig when I was twelve at a New Year's Eve house party. It was 1964 and I made a whopping $60.00. That was as much as some men made in a week in those days. After that I knew I had to make music a part of my life. Who would have thought you could have all that fun and get paid too.

February 12, 2011 I as inducted into the Rockabilly Hall of Fame. It was a special honor for me because I have so many close friends who have been inducted before me. I had a really neat gig for a few years playing with Eddie Bond. Eddie had some hits but decided to stay around the Mid South area rather than being on the road away from his family. He did make numerous trips overseas to Germany and other rockabilly markets in Europe. He had a TV show and was a well known and respected radio personality, owning several radio stations along the way. I was the staff drummer (cool word for a regular drummer) on his TV show for a while. During my stint with the "Stompers Band" I got to work with some big names and it was a lot of fun. As a matter of fact, our bass player, Pat Neal, was one of the original members of the Gentrys (Keep on Dancing). He also had a lot of rockabilly background. Also, Eddie's front man forever, Bobby Killingsworth (Cousin Bo Jack) was a great treat to work with. There was never a dull moment with that guy for sure. I also ran across one the most talented guitar/harp players as well as vocalists while working with Eddie Bond by the name of Jim Smith. He has helped out the "Live Wire Band" over the years and remains a great friend.

Skeet Seaton induction in the
Internet Rockabilly Hall of Fame
Bob Timmers, Skeet Seaton
Sunshine Sonny Payne, C.W. Gatlin

During the King Biscuit Blues
Festival, Helena, AR
at the Miller Hotel
Live Wire and Jim Smith
(center stage)

Larry Shirley, Tommy Darnell
Skeet Seaton, Allen Snider

Mellow Street Syndicate

Live Wire Band 2002
Tom Mathis, John Pope,
Skeet Seaton, Little Henry Edgin,
and the Bud Mobile

Live Wire Band at the Monroe Tavern
Henry Edgin, Matt Kelley, Skeet,
Jimmy Rogers, John Pope

I made my first TV appearance at the ripe old age of 12 on a popular show out of Little Rock, AR called "Eye on Arkansas." It was one of the few times I was ever nervous behind a set of drums. (I am old school and can't get used to drum kit.) The other time was when my good friend Levon Helm was standing about 5 feet behind me on the stage. As far as recording goes, I did my first session at Sonic Studio with my good friend, Jimmy Evans. Also on the session was C.W. Gatlin. That is where I first met Roland James. He is one of the nicest people you will meet in the music business (or anywhere else on this planet) and he has never gotten the recognition that he deserves. I did some recording with Mack Self and backed him up at the Arkansas Jamboree on his shows. I did a session at American Studios with Jimmy Evans. We recorded a song, Pink Cadillac (before the other Pink Cadillac). It did well on the overseas market and will probably be the biggest one I will ever play on.

Over the years I have played everything from the Memphis Coliseum to a pole shed at Holub Crossing, AR. I enjoyed every gig and have always tried to have a good band to be involved in. Over the years a lot of humorous things have occurred at gigs just as many other musicians have seen. I thought it would be interesting to share some of them and I realize some readers will not understand or appreciate the humor, but I am going to give it a shot. Of course, the names have been changed to protect the guilty.

In the Phillips International
recording studio with
Tom Mathis, Skeet Seaton and
engineer/musician Roland James

Arkansas Fallen Fire Fighter's
Memorial Motorcycle
Rally & Show
Forrest City, Arkansas

Who Called A Cab

It was a warm July night and the band was playing at the notorious Delta Supper Club. It was one of the oldest clubs in the entire delta region and would seat around 250 to 300 patrons if you got them squeezed in just right. They had two window air conditioners and three or four huge homemade box fans and none of it ever reached the bandstand. It was full of cigarette smoke and loose women and if you wore a white shirt it was yellow at the end of the gig and if you were lucky it might even have a dab of lipstick on it as well. I was standing outside on the parking lot with Abner, my guitar player, trying to get some fresh air and catch a breeze, if we should be lucky enough to have one. A taxi cab (the only one in town) pulled in front of the club and honked several times in an effort to summon his customer. After having no luck, he turned to Abner and me and in a very agitated voice asked if we knew who called a cab. We both told him we had no idea. He got out of the cab, slammed the door and started cussing and ranting about the fact that he did not have time to fool will a bunch of drunks. We finished the gig and as we were loading our equipment, I noticed the guy who had called the cab carrying the cab driver out over his shoulder and the cab driver was so drunk he had to be put in the back seat of his own cab and the guy who had called a cab had to drive him home.

All Aboard For Memphis

I had a gig in Blytheville, Arkansas at an Air Force base NCO club. I was a senior in high school and had never been out of Phillips County very often. The guitar player Ned was grown and had been around so he went with me and drove with the understanding I would pay attention and drive back. He had to be at work at 7 a.m. and I had no intention of making it to school the next day. Well, we played the gig, loaded up and headed home. He got me out of town and back to the interstate and then he went to sleep. I drove and drove and drove and all of a sudden I went across this big bridge I did not remember and then down into the middle of these huge buildings. It was then that Ned woke up, looked at this watch and knew we should be home. He looked around and said, " HOW THE HELL DID WE WIND UP IN MEMPHIS?"

The Ferry Boat Ride

I was playing in a four-piece honky tonk band and we had a booking in Dyersburg, TN. I was eighteen and I thought this was a major road gig. It turned out to be one, because the bridge was a long way from being thought about, much less built. We left around the middle of the afternoon and headed off on one of the craziest road trips ever made. When we got to the gig it was already beginning to thunder and lightning and by the time we got through playing, it had turned into a major thunderstorm. The whole band was pretty well wasted and it was a real chore getting packed up. It was strictly an old school gig. Four drunks in a pickup truck loaded down with band equipment and no clue how to find the ferry because it was raining so hard you could not see the end of the truck hood. It just gets better! We had about two thirds of our last fifth and Abner and I figured one more would not hurt anything at this point. Shortly after we got started on our cocktail, we accidentally found the ferry and he held up for us. I am quite sure he will always reflect upon that decision as one of his worst errors in judgment. Keep in mind that the rain was still pouring and the wind was really blowing. Abner and I decided to go up into the wheelhouse, so we bailed out of the pickup truck (with fifth in hand) and began our climb up the slippery steps. When we got to the top of the stairs, we opened the door and stepped into the wheelhouse. We looked like two drowned rats with a fifth of whiskey. We both had longhair and beards and from the reaction of the ferry captain, he was not impressed. I thought the best thing would be a peace offering, so in a gesture of friendship, I stuck out the fifth and offered him a shot of whiskey. What would be better on a cold wet night? He wasted little time in telling us we could not stay up there. We talked him into letting us stay until the rain slacked up, so we sat down and Abner started telling the guy he thought it was pretty cool to be able to pilot a ferry. We talked a little and soon the pilot broke down and had a social nip. Abner was telling him he was a truck driver and it shouldn't be any different driving the ferry. At this point, Abner asked if he could drive the ferry a little. The captain told Abner that he better not and Abner explained to the captain that all he had to do was follow that light out in front of the boat. The captain said, "you drunk s.o.b., that light is on the end of the boat." It was at that point that we felt the rain had slacked up enough for us to go back to the truck.

A.G. Seaton on
accordian

One Very Foggy Night

We were playing a New Year's Eve gig at the Sonny Boy Blues Hall in Helena, which is right on the banks of the Mississippi River. There was a fog that rolled in that night unlike any I have ever seen in my life. Because of the weather, the crowd was not nearly as good as we had hoped it would be. The band decided that we would help the small crowd bring in the New Year, seeing as how they had weathered the elements to come and hear us play. Archie was playing keyboard with us that night and he had a Fender Rhodes piano. For those who are not aware, it has four legs that screw into the bottom of the piano. During the course of the night, we drank large amounts of tequila (Jose) and we were really having a big time. Well, it soon became time to pack up and get out. I had driven Archie over in his car because the rest of us were coming back the next day to get our stuff. As I was packing my stuff, I could barely see a set of arms through the fog going up and down as if they were trying to flag down a car. I walked out and it was Archie trying to close the trunk of his car. I walked over and asked what the problem was and he informed me that he was having trouble closing his trunk lid. As I looked down, I noticed in his condition he had forgotten to screw the legs out of his piano. Maybe it was the fog??? On a final note, as we were driving to my house in his car, he looked at me and in a serious tone, asked me, "Do you think my car will be ok there overnight?"

Skeet Seaton and Jimmy Evans

Smoke Em If You Got Em

As if our first trip to Blytheville, AR wasn't bad enough, we headed back up there again about six weeks later to the same place. For some reason Ned thought it best if he drove. I had a rather unusual vehicle at the time. It was a 1962 Chevy two-door station wagon. We were making our way down the road with our windows down since I didn't have air conditioning. Ned thumped his cigarette out the window and about twenty minutes later we began to smell smoke. I looked in the back seat and it was flaming from Ned's cigarette. We quickly pulled over and luckily there was water in a road ditch so we took our pop bottles and filled them up and put out the fire. I told Ned, winding up in Memphis wasn't nearly as bad as trying to burn my car up.

Know Your Audience!

I had played a day gig at a festival in Mississippi and I had a friend of mine playing sax on the gig. I had a gig back in Arkansas later that same night and so after a few beers on the way back, Bubba, my sax man, decided he would go play the Arkansas gig with me. It was a small crowd and we were in the first set, so we decided to play some tunes we liked, such as Stranger on the Shore, Misty and so on. Not your regular honky tonk selections. We were in the middle of one of these tunes when some guy in a John Deere work shirt (a greasy one at that) walked up to the stage and wanted to know if we could play something without that damn saxophone in it. It was then that we knew we had to go back to our usual honky tonk tunes.

Live Wire at J.R. Bar & Grill
Southhaven, MS
Henry Edgin, John Pope,
Skeet, Rodney Jumper
Matt Kelley

Skeet and Gary Dixon on Harmonica

A Multi-talented musician and a great
guy to work with

Guess Who's Here

Davey and I were doing a live interview on the King Biscuit Time radio show at the Delta Cultural Center in Helena. There have been a lot of people who have just appeared there from time to time. Robert Plant is one that comes to mind. Well, right in the middle of our interview none other than Elvis Costello walks in and starts looking at all the things on display from old blues artists and rockabilly legends in the museum there. When Sonny Payne cut to commercial, he invited Elvis to come and be interviewed. He was very polite and didn't want to cut in on our time but we all insisted that he join us. He was doing some session work over in Mississippi and had a gig in Memphis that night. Helena was a small detour from his trip so he wanted to stop in and see what was going on. It was really neat the way it went from there. From the things he said on the air, it actually sounded like Elvis was playing with our band that night at our gig. He is a very nice person and it was a great honor to meet him. The real kicker to this story is that when his new CD came out, he put Davey and me on his list of dedications.

Little Henry Edgin, Terry Buckalew, Skeet Seaton & Elvis Costello

Early Eye Opener

We were playing a Christmas festival and the weather was a little nippy. I had a friend of mine come down and help us out. The gig started at eleven so we had to head that way around eight thirty. I asked Bill if he wanted to stop and get a ham and biscuit. Bill reached under the seat and brought out a pint and said that he had something that would be better on a cold morning and so I caved in and helped him with it. When we got to the gig it was time for a refill. We got another and played the gig. It turned out to look a lot like Christmas that day.

Skeet with Eddie Bond and Bo Jack (Dave Roe on bass)

The Eddie Bond Show

A Band for Gypsies

There was a large group of gypsies who moved into our area and they loved to party but had a bad reputation about not paying their bills. They booked us to play a party for them at the American Legion Hut. We agreed with the understanding that we would not hit the first note until we had the cash in hand. Once we started playing things got really out of hand. There were pictures of the past commanders of the Legion going all around the walls back to WWII. The kids were taking them down and throwing them like Frisbees. Somehow they got into the upstairs meeting room and got hold of some small flags and were using them to sword fight. There was a cake on a table and one of the little devils grabbed a handful of it and threw it on Abner's 1961 telecaster. I thought it was pretty funny until the next handful of cake hit the center of my bass drum head. The band quit in the middle of the song and told them that when they got the little monsters under control, we would start back. We had to take turns guarding the stage on break. At the end of the last set (and a few cocktails) they talked us into playing one more set. As we got to the last half of the last set we noticed that the only ones left were the women and monsters. As you might think, no one knew anything about more money. A few weeks later we were going to a men's store for band clothes (old school) and the gypsy king was coming out. (The king is the main cat) We cornered him up and were about to get our money or some other satisfaction when out of nowhere two carloads of family pulled up and that's when things went south. We decided to cut our losses and live to fight another day.

A Captured Audience (and band)

We have always played the county fair as I have mentioned in other stories. For several years the Cummings prison band would play as well. We would be on one end of the pavilion and they would be on the other end. We would take turns playing sets. After a few years we got to know the guys, however they sometimes had to change band members. One of the guys came down to us and said they had a new drummer who just started with them and he was not up on some of their tunes. Since we played some of the same material he wanted me to sit in with them on the next set and the new guy could listen. I already cleared it with the guard and it would be ok. I told him that there were two things they needed to understand. First of all, I was not wearing one of those white suits and second of all, I was damn sure not getting on the bus when they left. Well, as you might know as soon as we kicked off, here came a couple of my friends and after a second look one of them said, "I knew you would make it someday." It's so nice to have friends.

A Gay Old Time

We were booked on a club date for New Year's Eve back several years ago and it turned out the band got entertained as much as the crowd. It was a small venue (60 people) but the club owner really wanted us so he came across with the money. My regular keyboard man wound up having to work so I got a guy from Memphis at the last minute to play piano. The club owner was a super nice guy who would go out of his way to accommodate anyone. Well, as the night went on, a lot of women came in and we noticed that the dance floor started filling up with women. It soon became clear that we had been invaded by lesbians. They started putting on a show that would have cost a lot of money to see in New Orleans or any big city and we were getting to see it for free. The club owner did not really care about having all that going on in his club so he came out on the dance floor and was going to get them to sit down. The girls all grabbed him by the arms and legs and it wasn't long until he was on his back on the dance floor and the girls had him covered like ants on honey. We got through with the song and he restored order. …Meanwhile, the piano player's wife, who was sitting next to my wife, made it clear that her husband was not going to play if all that was going on. Luckily things settled down and we were able to finish with the band intact.

Fight Night

All musicians have played rough joints a time or two especially when we were paying our dues in our younger days. I was playing with some cats from Memphis. We had a kicking 3-piece band and the keyboard player also covered the bass line. We could really cook. We booked a skull orchard that was supposed to be toned down quite a bit. However, later in the night be found out differently. It was a Friday and Saturday gig and the first night was ok. There was a shoving match outside on Friday night, but what the heck. On the way back to do the Saturday gig we were talking about how it wasn't too bad and I might ask the lady who ran the club about booking us back in. We kicked off the first set and things went ok. There was a little tension between a group in the corner, but nothing serious. Well, when we started off the second set, all hell broke loose. I thought I was in a saloon fight in Dodge City. They were throwing each other over tables, hitting each other with chairs and fists. Well, so much for booking back in there. I said, "I just want to get out of here alive, and to hell with coming back!!!" About that time the Sheriff's department showed up in full force. One of the deputies came over and wanted to know who was in charge of the band. I really hated to tell him, but I confessed that I was. He informed me in no uncertain terms that we would be packing up and getting the hell out of there. He said as long as we were playing, they would never get it broken up. I explained that we were from Memphis and Helena and we hadn't been paid yet. He talked to the owner, came back with our money, and told us to start packing. We were carrying equipment in one hand and pushing people out of the way with the other.

Dead Drunk

We were playing a club in Mississippi that once was a plantation commissary. It had been turned into a club and it was a really neat place. We had a friend who followed the band around and he would pass out drunk from time to time. We hadn't played there before so we were sort of looking around the club. My lead singer, Davey, who was always pulling something on the unsuspecting spotted a wooden casket against the wall at the front of the club. Our friend had passed out, so we thought how funny it would be to put him in the casket. When we headed over to check it out everyone started looking and laughing and brought him back into the real world. He just did not have a clue what he was about to experience.

The Gig That Went to the Dogs

We had a guy call us to play a private party. He told me he had built a new shop building and wanted to break it in right. That was what we did best. When we got there it was a nice building but it was also full of four wheelers and dogs. Another thing that made it interesting was the fact that it was built right on a slough. There had to be at least three million mosquitoes per dog and they had a lot of them as well. We got everything set up and had a little time left before time to start the gig. We walked outside and heard a crash. The dogs had gotten back in the building after being tossed out. They all got tangled up in the microphone cords and pulled the mics down on the new concrete floor. After checking everything out, it seemed ok. As we started playing we would play with one hand and swat with the other. At the end of the night and a thousand bites later we started packing up and when we turned on the lights, the pretty new white concrete floor was solid black from mosquitoes that had been danced on.

Down at the 7-11

Gerald, who is one of my Memphis picking buddies, and I were playing a country music show that was a popular spot and it was a family type show. The manager made it clear that there was to be positively no alcohol. He didn't say anything about bringing it in after it was consumed, so I considered it a gray area. I drove to Gerald's house and was going to ride with him. He had a new truck and I asked if I could drive it and he let me know that would never happen. As we made our way down the road a pint of Southern Comfort appeared. Gerald knew a short cut so we cut through a small town and got back on the main road. I am telling you this because it became a major problem later. We made quick work of the pint, so we stopped and figured a fifth would be better. We had a snort or two out of it and were soon at the gig, which somehow went off ok. We were on our way back and halfway through the fifth and all of a sudden Gerald pulled over, threw open the door and started throwing up. He was really in a bad way. All of a sudden the new truck that I would never drive was under my complete control and so was Gerald. I was driving down the highway with one hand and holding him by the collar with the other as he leans out the door trying to rid his body of the devil's poison. I only knew one way to get to Gerald's and it was not the way he took us. I figured this was going to be a major ordeal so I pulled into some town at a 7-11 to get coffee and something to eat. For some reason, Gerald decided to get out and go behind the store instead of going in to the restroom.

I had to get something fast, so I just let him go. I saw his big feet go up in the air as I was going in, but I didn't have time to fool with him. On top of everything else, I had another captain working for me till I could get back to the fire station in West Helena, which at that particular moment seemed 1,000 away. I came back out and put my stuff in the new truck I would never drive and went around to get Gerald and get out of town. Well, when I got around there, Gerald was not to be found. In the back of my mind, I am thinking, "This drunk s.o.b. has wandered off and we are both heading to jail in a short time." As I stood there gathering my thoughts on how to avoid jail, I hear a groan and a desperate cry for help. Due to the shock of Gerald not being there and the pitch darkness of the night I had failed to notice a 6 foot deep drainage ditch which seemed to hold Gerald in it's grasp. I am not a very big guy and Gerald was not a very small guy, so things were not as easy as I would have liked. I climbed down halfway, grabbed him by the arm, and with a lot of tugging and cussing, I managed to rescue my partner in crime and escape jail. As I headed out to take my friend home, I had to go all the way around on the 240 loop, which was about thirty five minutes longer than the trip to the gig. About half way around the interstate Gerald decides he needs some more relief, so once again I am driving the truck I would never drive with one hand, holding him be the neck with the other. When I finally got him home, I left him slumped over in his front seat, jumped in my truck and headed to the fire station. The next day I got a call from Gerald wanting to know what I had done to him, his truck and where he lost a three thousand dollar diamond out of his ring.

Something Different

All of my gigs have not necessarily been crazy. I have been honored on several occasions to perform at very prestigious performances. I played on the 15,000th broadcast of the King Biscuit Time radio show on KFFA. It is the longest running live blues show in the nation. We performed as well as Robert Lockwood, Jr. and Gene Schwartz, who has been playing with Lockwood for years. Robert Lockwood Jr. was one of the original King Biscuit Time players along with Sonny Boy Williamson. The 15,000th broadcast was held at the old movie theatre in Helena, which has been renovated, and it is a really nice venue. The show was broadcast via the Internet so blues fans worldwide got to hear it. It was also an honor to be on stage with my long time friend Sonny Payne who emceed the show.

Skeet playing at the 15,000th King Biscuit Time show at the Malco Theater, Helena, AR

Gene Schwartz, Robert Lockwood, Jr.
Skeet Seaton, C.W. Gatlin, Jim Howe
Ed Burks, Sonny Payne, Sam Carr

15,000th King Biscuit Time Show

We Blew Em Away

We were booked at a club up north about 100 miles. We knew that there was going to be some rough weather but we didn't know it was going to be as rough as it got. We got about 30 miles from the gig and a tornado hit just 10 miles from us. We pulled under a canopy at a truck stop to escape the hail, and waited out the storm. When we got to the club, they were sweeping water out the front door of the club. We went ahead and set up to play and we wound up with two women who weathered the storm. At the end of the second set, the club owner said to call it a night and cut our money, which we did not argue about since the weather was still kind of rough and we were ready to be home. We had a keyboard player who had been with us for about three weeks and had just bought an expensive amp. We did not make much money that night and Buddy made the comment that it was going to take a long time to pay for that amp at this rate.

We Take Tips

We were playing at a VFW in a small town not far from home and we had a bass player who was usually pretty quiet, but once in a while he would get sideways. We had just come back off break and Junior got on the mic and made the following announcement, "We do take requests when accompanied by a dollar bill. We even take food stamps." In just a few minutes a little lady came across the dance floor, handed Junior a food stamp and asked to hear "It's Crying Time Again." Junior never did give us our cut from that now that I think about it.

Fast forward to the same club about eight years later with a different band. We were asked to play over, so they passed a John Deere hat around to see what they could come up with for another set. When we checked it out, there was enough cash and in the bottom of the hat was a gold man's wedding ring. It was either someone who was getting divorced or somebody tried to hide it and threw it in by mistake along with some money. (If so, someone had some explaining to do the next morning!!!) Davey snatched the ring and said he would take it and we could split the money among the rest of the band. That sounded fine to us cause most of us had several wedding bands of our own. We wound up with an extra sixty bucks apiece. Well, Davey couldn't wait to get to the jewelry store first thing Monday morning to see how good a deal he had pulled off. The jeweler looked at it and told Davey it was worth about five bucks and he was not interested in buying it.

Creepy Crawlers

VFW's seem to be the place to see weird stuff. We were playing at one a few years back and a guy came in and seemed to be causing a real scene. We took a break and I went up to the bar at the front of the club. It was then I found out what the deal was. This guy was walking around with a small rattlesnake wrapped around his arm while holding it by the neck. He was asked to leave and take his guest with him. I found out a day or two later that he had left in his truck and got bitten by the snake. He woke up in serious trouble!

Who's Next?

After retiring from the fire department, I got my barber's license. We were playing a club and acquired some new fans. I don't have much hair, so in the last few years, I have shaved my head. One of these guys in our new group of fans would get in his cups and make the comment that he wanted to be like me when he grew up. I told him if he wanted to be like me he would have to have a haircut like mine. He told me to get my clippers and get with it. What he didn't know is that I happened to have them with me in my truck. I went out and got them and came back into the club. I put him in a chair, unplugged a beer sign and plugged in my clippers, and went to work. I went right down the middle of his head and down to the skin so there was no backing out. The bar owner came over, looked at what I was doing and said, "I have been running a bar a long time, but I ain't never seen anything like this."

Can You Play a Shuffle?

Rose and I were in a well-known club called Flora-Bama, down on the Florida and Alabama state line. It is a really cool place and they have live music. I was sitting on the second level enjoying the music. It was a three-piece band and they were sounding good. I had on some type of drummer shirt and when the band took a break, the drummer stopped by to talk to me. He was a younger cat, just getting started and he asked me if I could play a shuffle. He wanted me to sit in and do a couple of tunes so he could check it out. Shuffles are a standard style of drumming in this area and I had a blast playing with the band. (The Flaming Iguanas) He was pleased to get the exposure to a new drum style for him, so it was a fun night for everyone.

The Seaton Hot Shots

Stage Dedication

As I said earlier, I have been involved in a lot of events that were of importance to our local community. One such gig was for the dedication of a new stage built in downtown Helena to be used for the King Biscuit Blues Festival and many other local events.

Another big occasion was to celebrate the consolidation of the two cities (Helena/West Helena). My band played for the big consolidation party at the old renovated train station in downtown Helena. There were all of the local politicians as well as all of the supporters at the event and this being my hometown, it was nice to be a part of this historic occasion.

Shoot Out At Shadden's

There was a place down the road a bit that was a world acclaimed **BBQ** place. When you pulled up and looked at the place you began to have second thoughts about eating there. It was an old country store building at least 80 years old and it looked every day of it. The **BBQ** was the best you ever wrapped your lips around. When the duck hunters came in for their hunts, we would go down to Shadden's and lay some good ole delta blues on them. One night my guitar player was in his gunslinger mood and had a 38 stuck in his waistband. After the gig, the store owner, who we had known for years, and the two of us were settling up when the store owner pulled an old dusty and rusty pistol out from under the counter and proceeded to tell us that he had plenty of protection. At this point, Abner looked him straight in the eye and said "BUT WILL IT DO THIS?" Abner pulled out his 38 and shot a hole in the old stained ceiling. Dirt and dust fell from the bullet hole for what seemed like at least 30 minutes. Jake looked at Abner and said "WE HAVE BEEN FRIENDS FOR A LONG TIME YOU S.O.B. BUT DON'T EVER DO THAT AGAIN!" At that point, we loaded up and headed back home.

Dead Dumpster

We were playing a blues gig at the old Holiday Inn in Helena and Abner was still acting like Wyatt Earp. After we got through he went out and got in the truck while I squared up with the boss. As I came out the back door, I heard a couple of gunshots and hurried to see what the problem was. You never knew what to expect from Abner. When I got there, he had fired two fatal shots and killed the Holiday Inn dumpster. He showed no remorse. I jumped behind the wheel of his truck, loaded him up, and got out of there before someone called the law. As we were going down the highway, he fired off three more rounds at signs. I knew it was ok then because he only had 5 shots. As he looked at me with a devilish grin, he opened the glove box and what did I see? A new box of 38 shells. It was the longest 2 miles I have ever driven.

Cotton Club Blackout

My band was playing at a club in Brinkley and we had a really good crowd. We were in the middle of a rocking tune when all of a sudden, the power went off and we were in total darkness. We waited for a minute or two but the lights never came back on. At this point the club owner came over and told us the power was off all over town and the power company said it could be as much as 2 hours before it would be restored. He wasn't happy but said to come to the bar and he would pay me. On my way to the bar I saw a really crazy thing. There were two guys shooting pool in the dark and they would pass a flashlight back and forth as they took turns shooting. What a crazy night.

Dog Dancing

We play a small club not far from home that has been there as long as I can remember. It is one of our favorite juke joints to play. There is a wide range in age, so we play a mix of music styles. There are still a few of the older hanger on-ers that drop in once in a while. One such fellow is an older tall skinny man with a really bad hump back. He always dances bare footed regardless of the time of year, wears overalls and a floppy hat. We were playing at this particular joint one night and it was really crowded. We were playing a nice slow belly rubber when Davey looked at me and nodded toward the dance floor, which at that time had about forty or fifty people on it. I looked around and there is the old fella mentioned above holding a large mixed breed dog by the front paws while it was standing on its back legs. The old guy was smiling like he was dancing with Madonna. As soon as the song was over I told Davy, "This place is going to the dogs!"

The Big Time

I remember the first time I ever played at the Peabody Hotel in Memphis. I was really excited to be playing at such a highbrow venue. That was until I had to unload. I don't know how many people reading this have ever played there, but you have to unload at the back door and work your equipment through the kitchen while they are trying to do their thing in there. Once you clear the kitchen, then you have to catch a freight elevator and go to whichever ballroom you are playing and unload. If all you have is a guitar and amp, you are fine, but let's face it, if you are a drummer, you have to make several trips and by the time you have unloaded all your drum gear, you know the chef by his first name and all of his kids too. Then after the gig you have to do it all in reverse.

Someone Call the Sheriff

A guy who owned a restaurant decided to put a small club in the back. He hired a friend to play, not knowing he didn't have a regular band. So, like most of us have at one time or another, he took the gig and then got a band together. (It's not foolproof, but sometimes it works.) A friend named Hank who played lead guitar and I decided to do it that weekend so we went up and played Friday night and we were supposed to be back Saturday night. Meanwhile, a guy who owned a club in town needed a drummer and a guitar man to play in his house band. He wanted us and we told him it would be next week. He said that whoever started would have first shot. Since the other gig was just a one-time deal, and the new one was three times a week, it was a no brainer. The gig wasn't booked in our names anyway. Hank and I went to pick up our gear and the club owner came in while we were packing up and wanted to know what the hell we thought we were doing. We explained that we were not part of this guy's band and he said he didn't give a damn. We were booked there and we couldn't get our stuff until after the gig and we wouldn't have to pack it up because he would throw the shit out in the parking lot. He was a pretty good-sized guy. We called the other club's manager and told him the situation. He told us to hold tight, and in about ten minutes, the phone rang. We could tell by his side of the conversation that it was about us. I had forgotten that our new boss' nephew was the sheriff of that county and he informed the owner that it would be in his best interest to give us our stuff with no more problems. When he hung up, he was not happy and told us to get our shit out of this place and he would be back in thirty minutes. If we were still there when he got back, sheriff or no sheriff, there would be hell to pay. Needless to say, it was the only time I ever had a guitar player help me pack up my drums!!!

The Seaton Hot Shots

Going Down

I booked a club once that I had heard about but had not played there or for that matter, I had never been in it. When we got there we discovered it was down two flights of stairs under an old car dealership. The stairs were very narrow and steep, and once you got to the first landing and went down to the final landing, you had to make a sharp left turn into the club. You then had to carry all of your equipment through the entire club to get to the bandstand at the back of the club. It was then that I realized I might have booked this gig a little too cheaply. We played the gig and had a good time. Then we realized what was ahead, carrying all that equipment through all the drunks and back up those awful stairs. One of our friends used to follow the band and was an unofficial roadie at times. When we finally got all that stuff back up and packed in the trailer, our friend turned in his notice that he was no longer in the roadie business.

Tri County Fair

We have a county fair that has been going on since before WWII and around 10 years ago it became the Tri-County fair by putting the three surrounding counties of Phillips, Lee and Monroe together. It always opens on Labor Day Monday and the temperature is never below 95 degrees. It is sort of a break from the club scene that we mostly play. There is always livestock on hand, quilting, jelly and jams and the usual fair stuff along the midway. I have been doing this fair gig for around seventeen years and have seen a lot of sights. We have a pretty good following each year. The fair committee hired an Elvis impersonator one time that used canned music. From time to time the can would roll away from him and he would have to catch up. Each year his Elvis suit shrank (or Elvis grew) and he quit doing the gig. He either didn't have the money to get a new suit or he moved on to Graceland...

At the Tri County Fair
Marvell, AR

Live Wire Band at the
Elaine Country Christmas
Henry Edgin, John Pope,
Jimmy Rogers, Skeet, Matt Kelley

The Eddie Bond Show

There was a cat in Memphis by the name of Eddie Bond whose name was a household word in the Mid South area when it came to rockabilly and country music. He was also a well-known DJ and owned several radio stations himself. He had a popular TV show that was broadcast from Memphis. I played on the show a while and it was a real hoot and a fun new experience. We would tape three shows at each recording session and the station would air one each Saturday morning. A guy would reset the clock on the wall behind my drums to 6 a.m. at the beginning of each show to make it look like we were live on the air. By being in "The Stomper Band," I worked with big name people and really made a lot of friends in the music business.

Eddie Bond's Show

Skeet and Jeannie Seely

Catfish & Minnows

I like to play music and I don't really care where I play it. One of my band buddies, Davey, is just as bad. I booked a little grocery store over in Mississippi that sits at a crossroads on Highway 1. They sold fishing bait, made burgers and had really cold beer. On Friday nights the lady who owned the store would cook up some of the best catfish and trimmings you ever tasted. She asked me if I could get someone to come over and play some music with me. The only problem was that it was a very small store, so we wound up playing on top of the minnow vat. It was a fun gig and we wound up playing there several more times.

Henry Edgin, Tom Mathis
Skeet, Jimmy Rogers

Nashville Drum Fiasco

We were doing a pretty big show in Nashville and our band was opening for a major act. Gerald had worked with some big artists and he knew the road manager for this act. He asked if I could play his drummer's set and he said ok. Well, I take off to Music City with nothing but a stick bag. When we got there, the main act had already set up and the rest of the band I was with set up around them. I walked up to the drummer and introduced myself and told him what I had been told about playing his drums. He very quickly told me no one was playing on his drums. Well, here I am with a stick bag and a confused look (nothing new). I went over to Gerald and explained the situation. We both walked over to the guy and Gerald told him the deal with his road manager and he said he didn't allow anyone to play his stuff. Time is running short by now so Gerald tells him that his corporation is putting on the convention and I was not a beginner and if anything happened they would take care of it. The answer was still no. At this point Gerald told him that he left him no choice. He would rent me a set and he could tear his down and explain to his boss why he had to wait to come on stage because he wasn't set up yet. All of a sudden it didn't really seem to be as much of a problem and I thanked him when I got off the drum throne and we all lived happily ever after....

Tequila Anyone?

I must admit that we play good dance music but at times we can be a bit of a party band. We were doing a gig at a neat little club in southern Arkansas and they had a really nice bandstand with a wide wooden rail around it. We were rocking along and a few of Davey's friends stumbled into the joint. Now anybody that knows Davey more than twenty minutes also knows that tequila is Davey's number one weakness. As the night progressed so did the empty shot glasses. When we got ready to leave we figured out what the rail was for. I kid you not, there were at least sixty empty shot glasses stacked up on the stage rail. The rail also kept Davey from falling off the stage. The key is to get drunk with the crowd and they never know the difference. I don't know if we were the cause or not, but the next time we played there the rail was gone.

Yellow Stone (not the park)

Back in the early 70's we were doing some sessions in a remote studio in a small town in Mississippi. We were right on the edge of stardom, or so we thought. We were playing Wednesday, Friday and Saturday and then we would drive to Mississippi to work on our tunes. Abner and I always needed a taste to limber us up and since we forgot to buy up for Sunday, we had to go see the nearest bootlegger. It wasn't a big chore since we knew exactly where he was. Well, he had Yellowstone half-pints. It was already 10:30 in the morning so we decided to have a small nip. We had nipped the first half pint plum up when we got to the studio. Now remember, it was a small town. There was a sewer ditch in front of the studio with a plank to cross the ditch. Well, as we were crossing the plank the last half pink slipped out of my hand into the ditch and went down to the bottom. Abner had a look that you see in horror flicks. We didn't want it then but about an hour later we were out there with a shovel retrieving our precious liquid. About a month later the IRS shut down the studio and our hit record could not be rescued like the Yellowstone half pint had been.

Bandstand High Dive

We were down in south Arkansas doing a gig and our regular bass player was on vacation. Buddy, who played piano and guitar was going to cover Peter's job on bass. We were almost through setting up when Buddy hung his flip-flop on a speaker cable and did a half gainer off the bandstand. Davey, who is never short on words, told Buddy, "That's what you get for wearing safety shoes." The whole band fell out laughing, however, Buddy saw little humor in the comment. As the night went on Buddy's elbow got bigger and bigger. Davey and Darrell wound up swapping out bass and we got through the gig but the sound was not up to our usual level. The next day Buddy found out he had a chipped elbow and had to have surgery plus he wasn't able to play for about a month.

Live Wire Band 2010
Matt Kelley, John Pope,
Rodney Jumper, Skeet
Little Henry Edgin

Nice Boots

I hired a guy to play with the band that I hadn't seen in at least four years. The last time I played with him, he wouldn't play bars, however this time he said he would help me out. When we went to the gig and were setting up our equipment, I told Davey in advance that Jeff did not drink. Davey was going to get us a drink and asked Jeff if he wanted a coke. Jeff said to just bring him a beer and Davey gave me a what the hell look. Jeff had on a really nice new pair of cowboy boots. The band was on break and someone sent a whole tray of tequila shooters to the band and we had already had enough, so we told a guy sitting at our table that he could have them if he would drink them all at once. He grabbed that tray like it was full of diamonds. He drank all five shots in a row and then turned around and threw up all over Jeff's new boots. All I could say was, "Welcome to the band."

Can You Turn It Down?

Gerald called one Saturday and wanted to know if Davey and I could come up and help on a gig at a senior's club. We loaded up and headed that way. When we got there and set up we noticed that the youngest person up there besides the band was around 70 years old. We kicked off the show and as soon as we hit the last note of the first song, they wanted us to turn down. We turned down and made another pass at it and once again, we were too loud. They were all two stepping and an older gentleman came up and asked my wife to dance. He said his wife's hip was broken and she was on a walker and couldn't dance, but she wouldn't mind if he danced with her. A little later my wife was walking by the refreshment table and she saw one of the ladies look at her watch and say, "Oh my god, it's nine o'clock." As soon as word of the late hour made it's way through the crowd, they all grabbed their walkers and purses and the place was cleared out. Davey had already started playing unplugged and I was down to brushes. It was an interesting night at the International Harvester Hall in Frasier.

Two Man Brawl

At one of the engagements we were doing a Friday and Saturday night and usually Fridays were a little slow. It could be a little rowdy from time to time. They had a new bouncer and none of us had ever seen him in action. We were almost through for the night and there were only two guys left at the bar. All of a sudden they got into a fight with each other. Peter our bass player has a strange sense of humor at times and he looked at me and said, "Everybody in here is fighting." The new bouncer didn't fare too well either. He got in between the two guys and they both wound up beating him up. He didn't show up for work the next night and we got word that he had hung up his bouncer shoes.

Skeet and Bluesman Sam Carr

Legendary Blues Drummer

Peter and His Invincible Car

When you are out in the wee hours of the morning, you see a lot of strange things. That is not the real problem, however. The real problem is what you don't see. Our bass player Peter holds the band record for running over animals. I told him that if he kept it up PETA was going to ban us from playing. One night he ran over a deer and did quite a bit of damage to his car. Not long ago he was going home and a mule ran into the side of his car. Once again, it did a lot of damage and when it was all over, the guy put the mule back up by sticking a piece of barbed wire back into the post. It was the third time the mule had been hit by a vehicle. The only other thing we didn't see soon enough was the wild pig my wife hit with my new truck. Luckily it was a small pig and it bounced around under my truck, came out the back, and hit the corner of my band trailer. Another time, my wife was driving home and a drunk driver crossed the centerline and hit us, flipping the band trailer and totaling our Jeep Cherokee as well. It can get dangerous just trying to get home.

Return of the Dog Dancer

I told a story about a guy dancing with his dog a little earlier in the book. It was about five years ago. Well, guess what! We were playing for a birthday party/crawfish gig at a tractor shed in Turkey Scratch, AR. (Don't laugh; it is the home of my mentor, Levon Helm.) Lo and behold who should show up but the dog dancer! As soon as he got there and found out we were playing he was ready to rock. He brought in a picture that someone had taken of him dancing with his dog. I told him about my book and asked if I could borrow the picture to copy and hopefully put it in my book. He told me the sad news that his dog had passed away but that he had another new dog now. I asked if he had taught it to dance. He looked at me and said, are you ready for this? "I can't dance with it, THIS IS A BOY DOG."

Dog Dancer

Live Wire Band 2008
John Pope, Little Henry Edgin,
Alvin Self, Skeet Seaton

Skeet and bluesman
Charlie Musselwhite

The Band Started Back

When you play country clubs, catholic weddings, or whatever the gig might be, there is usually booze involved. Sometimes it causes trouble, but most of the time, it just adds fun to the occasion. This story I am about to tell is about one fella at a private party in Mississippi back when I was just getting started playing music. We had finished a gig and this particular guy was just having a great time and wasn't ready to go home. I was putting my cymbals in their bag and one slipped out and hit the floor with a loud crash. The guy grabbed his wife, started dancing and hollered out, "Alright, the band has started back up!"

Baltimore Bluesman

You meet a lot of musicians in a lot of different ways. I had a guy come into my barbershop and ask for Skeet Seaton. I sometimes wonder about the past popping up, but I said, "You're looking at him." He told me he had been down here on a visit and had been a guest on the King Biscuit Time radio show with Sonny Payne. After the show, he asked Sonny where he could get a haircut and Sonny directed him to my shop. As I was cutting his hair, we were talking about music and he seemed to have his heart in the right place. After I finished with his haircut, he went outside and brought in his axe. A real nice left-handed National. He played a few tunes and we talked a little and I invited him out to my house the next night. I have a music room in my house where I keep a set of 1959 Ludwig drums, a bass rig, a guitar rig and a small p.a. set up all the time for these sort of occasions. We all jammed for a couple of hours and we had a great time. His real name is John Pappajohn and he doesn't care to hear any pizza jokes.

C.W. Gatlin, Skeet Seaton
John Papajohn

Guess Who's Coming To Play?

My wife Rose and I host two parties each year and my band, along with bunches of other cats I have worked with over the years all show up to jam. We usually have anywhere from 60 to 80 people show up and one year I think we may have even broken 100. I am telling you this to get back to my point of how you meet new musical friends without knowing it is about to happen. We were having one of our parties and there were people scattered all over the yard. I was taking a break while someone else played drums for a while and I see this guy walking across my yard. Someone I don't know at all. I asked him if I could help him and he asked for Skeet. This really shocked me since I had no clue who this cat was. I introduced myself. He told me that a local guy that I play with sometimes told him about our party (it is rather a well known happening) and so he was wondering if he could come out and jam with us. I asked him what he played and he told me he was a harp man. I already had one of the best on the harp jamming as we spoke and I figured he could use a break, so I told him to grab his stuff and come on and dive in. I know most of you young guys won't know what I am talking about but he came out with a old carry case like the TV repair guys had where the top flips over on both sides. Man this cat had every harp known to man. We had a great time and I have no idea what his name was. It was one of those moments when a bunch of talented guys got together and it all gelled.

At another one of our get togethers, this guy showed up with a saxophone, walks in and goes to playing and I didn't even know he was there until I heard him. It really blew my mind hearing a sax that wasn't supposed to be there. He was from Branson, Missouri and had heard about our party from someone and thought he would stop by.

Skeet and Brent Foster

Keyboard (B3) man from Mt. View, AR
One of the Best!

The Things You See!!!!!

I had stopped off on my way to a gig to say Hi to some guys I knew from Nashville who were down here doing a blues gig. They were loading in and setting up. As I looked around, I noticed a one armed midget who was helping out and I assumed he was part of the road crew. Boy, was I ever wrong. Once they got the drums set up, this guy goes over and reaches into a box and pulls out a leather sleeve with a drumstick made into the end of it. It was laced kinda like a boxing glove. I watched with great interest as someone helped him get it on and lace it up. He then got behind the drums and began playing a little and it really brought a warm feeling into your heart to know that he overcame his disabilities and was doing what we all love to do. Play music. It also taught me not to make hasty judgments about people's abilities on first appearances. You never know what you will see next.

A.G. Seaton on piano
Robert "Duke" Snyder
on guitar

C.W. Gatlin, Skeet Seaton,
Rose Seaton, Ed Burks

Skeet performing at the
Delta Cultural Center
Helena, AR

Can You Say Roadblock?

Porter and I were heading to a gig one night in my old pickup truck sipping on a cold one and just having a big time. Porter looked down the road and told me to watch my speed there were blue lights ahead. All of a sudden Porter said that there must be wreck because there were a couple of police cars. Then came the words nobody wanted to hear. It's a damn roadblock! We started sticking empty beer cans under the truck seat as we rolled up to the intersection. I was still on the fire department and I knew most of the state troopers in our area, but guess what, I didn't know a single one of these guys. I carried a wallet badge from the fire department, and it wasn't very often a cop would ticket a firefighter. As I reached for my wallet, my foot slipped off the clutch and my old truck motor died. When the trooper walked up to my window, I made damn sure he saw my badge. He looked at my license and I tried to crank my old truck but to no avail. He looked at me and said, "I know you are a firemen and can't afford much more. I can't check your lights when it won't even start." Then he asked me if I knew how to clutch start it. I said sure I do and the next thing I know I have four state troopers in uniform pushing my truck and every time I popped the clutch the beer cans would roll out from under the seat. It finally fired off and I stuck my hand out the window and waved thanks to the troopers. Porter looked at me and said, "Damn, I ain't never seen nothing like that." I told him it was just our tax dollars at work. We popped another top and went on to the gig.

C.W. Gatlin, Jim Howe,
Skeet Seaton, Ed Burks

Musicians are a kind-hearted bunch as a general rule and benefits are performed from time to time. My band is the first to step up to the plate. A few years ago my son came down with a very rare illness and was having both sickness and financial trouble. We held a benefit for him. You just don't know how many friends you really do have until you need them. The community in general, as well as at least 40 musicians showed up and were very generous with their time, talent and support. It makes your heart feel good to know that there are still good people among us!

Local musicians at
Horses and Harley's Club
West Helena, AR

The Delta's best Musicians

The Next Forty Plus Years

I hope you enjoyed my little stories and maybe you will be around for the sequel. I know I hope I am. All of the stories are true and told to the best of my memory. As I said before if you have never stepped on stage and helped make people's lives happier by doing your best to entertain them to the best of your ability, you don't know what you have missed.

Made in the USA
Charleston, SC
23 November 2012